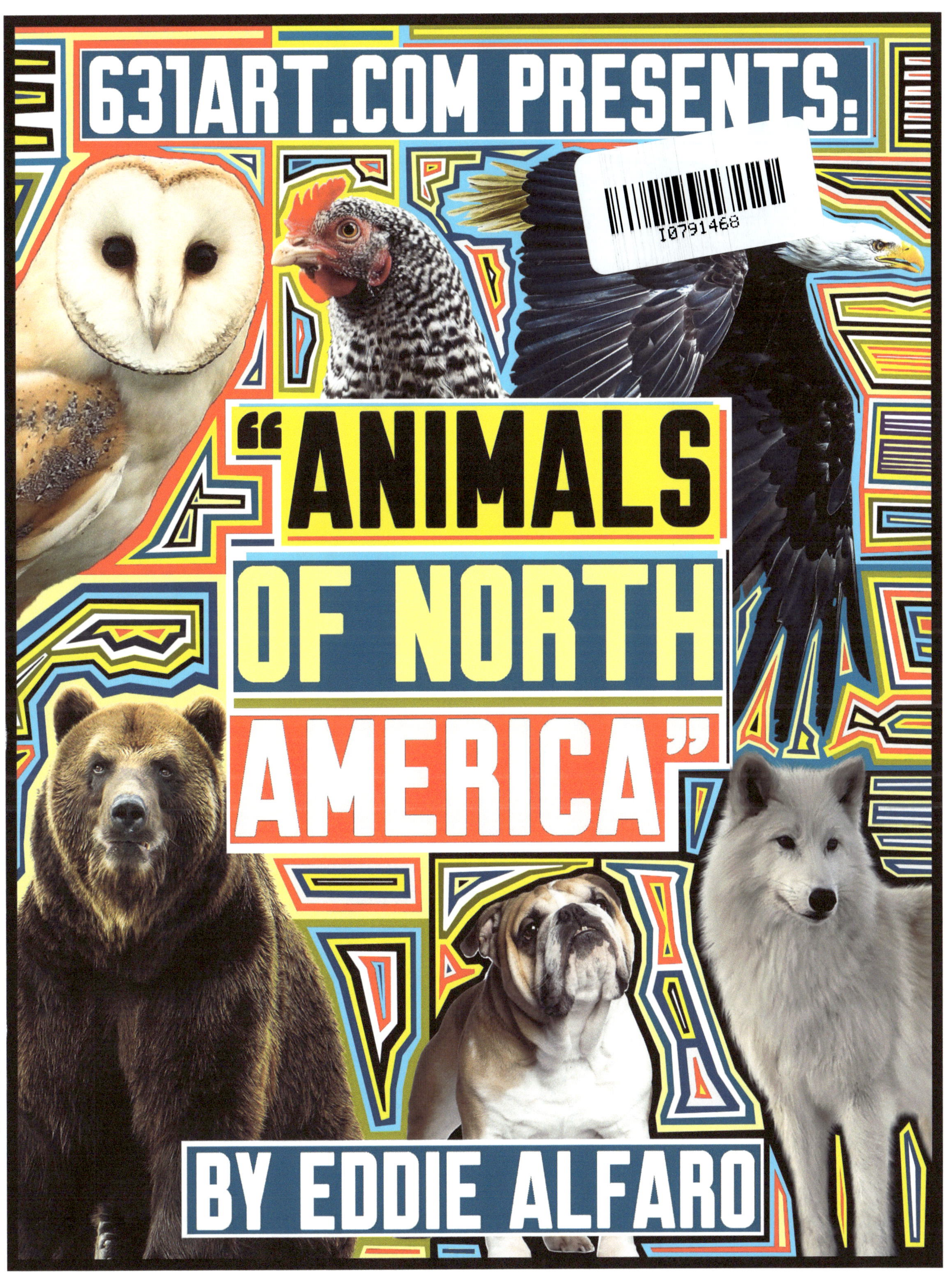
631ART.COM PRESENTS:
I0791468
"ANIMALS
OF NORTH
AMERICA"
BY EDDIE ALFARO

THE WOLF IS THE LARGEST MEMBER OF THE DOG FAMILY. WOLVES ARE LEGENDARY FOR THEIR HOWL, WHICH IS USED TO COMMUNICATE. A WOLF HOWLS TO ATTRACT THE ATTENTION OF THE PACK, WHILE A GROUP HOWL MAY SEND TERRITORIAL MESSAGES FROM ONE PACK TO ANOTHER.

RACCOONS CAN MAKE OVER FIFTY DIFFERENT SOUNDS TO COMMUNICATE! RACCOONS CAN HISS, PURR AND GROWL.

BROWN BEARS AREN'T JUST BROWN. SOME ARE CREAM OR BLACK. THEY DIG CAVES WITH THEIR LONG CLAWS. BROWN BEARS SLEEP IN THE CAVES FOR MOST OF THE WINTER.

THERE ARE OVER 60 DIFFERENT
SPECIES OF DEER WORLDWIDE.
A MALE DEER IS CALLED A BUCK
BUT SOME LARGER MALES ARE
REFERRED TO AS STAGS.

SEA OTTERS EAT 25 PERCENT OF THEIR BODY WEIGHT IN FOOD EVERY DAY.

FOXES HAVE WHISKERS ON THEIR LEGS AND
FACE, WHICH HELP THEM TO NAVIGATE.

IN THE ALGONQUIN LANGUAGE,
MOOSE MEANS EATER OF TWIGS.

THE BALD EAGLE HAS BEEN
THE NATIONAL EMBLEM OF
THE UNITED STATES SINCE 1782.

BROWN BEAR FEMALES HAVE BABIES
DURING THE WINTER IN THEIR SLEEP!

A GROUP OF OWLS IS CALLED A PARLIAMENT.

WORLD WAR I PROPAGANDA POSTERS WOULD ADOPT THE IMAGES
OF DOGS TO SYMBOLIZE DIFFERENT COUNTRIES. THE UNITED STATES
WAS REPRESENTED BY THE PIT BULL. THEY ARE RESPECTED FOR
THEIR LOYALTY, DETERMINATION, AND BRAVERY.

ROOSTERS PERFORM A DANCE CALLED TIDBITTING IN WHICH THEY MAKE 'TOOK, TOOK' FOOD CALLS TO LET OTHER CHICKENS KNOW OF THE PRESENCE OF FOOD.

KINGFISHERS HAVE A HARD BEAK
LIKE A DAGGER FOR SPEARING FISH.
KINGFISHER

HORSES CAN SLEEP BOTH LYING
DOWN AND STANDING UP.

POLAR BEARS HAVE BLACK SKIN AND ALTHOUGH THEIR FUR APPEARS WHITE, IT IS ACTUALLY TRANSPARENT.
POLAR BEAR

SWANS ARE AMONG
THE LARGEST FLYING BIRDS.

VULTURES HAVE EXCELLENT SENSES OF SIGHT AND SMELL TO HELP THEM LOCATE FOOD, AND THEY CAN FIND FOOD FROM A MILE OR MORE AWAY.
VULTURE

PIGS CAN'T SWEAT.

RABBITS PERFORM AN ATHLETIC LEAP,
KNOWN AS A 'BINKY', WHEN THEY'RE HAPPY,
DOING TWISTS AND KICKS IN MID AIR!

TURTLES DATE BACK TO THE TIME OF THE DINOSAURS, OVER 200 MILLION YEARS AGO!

THANK YOU.
THE END.

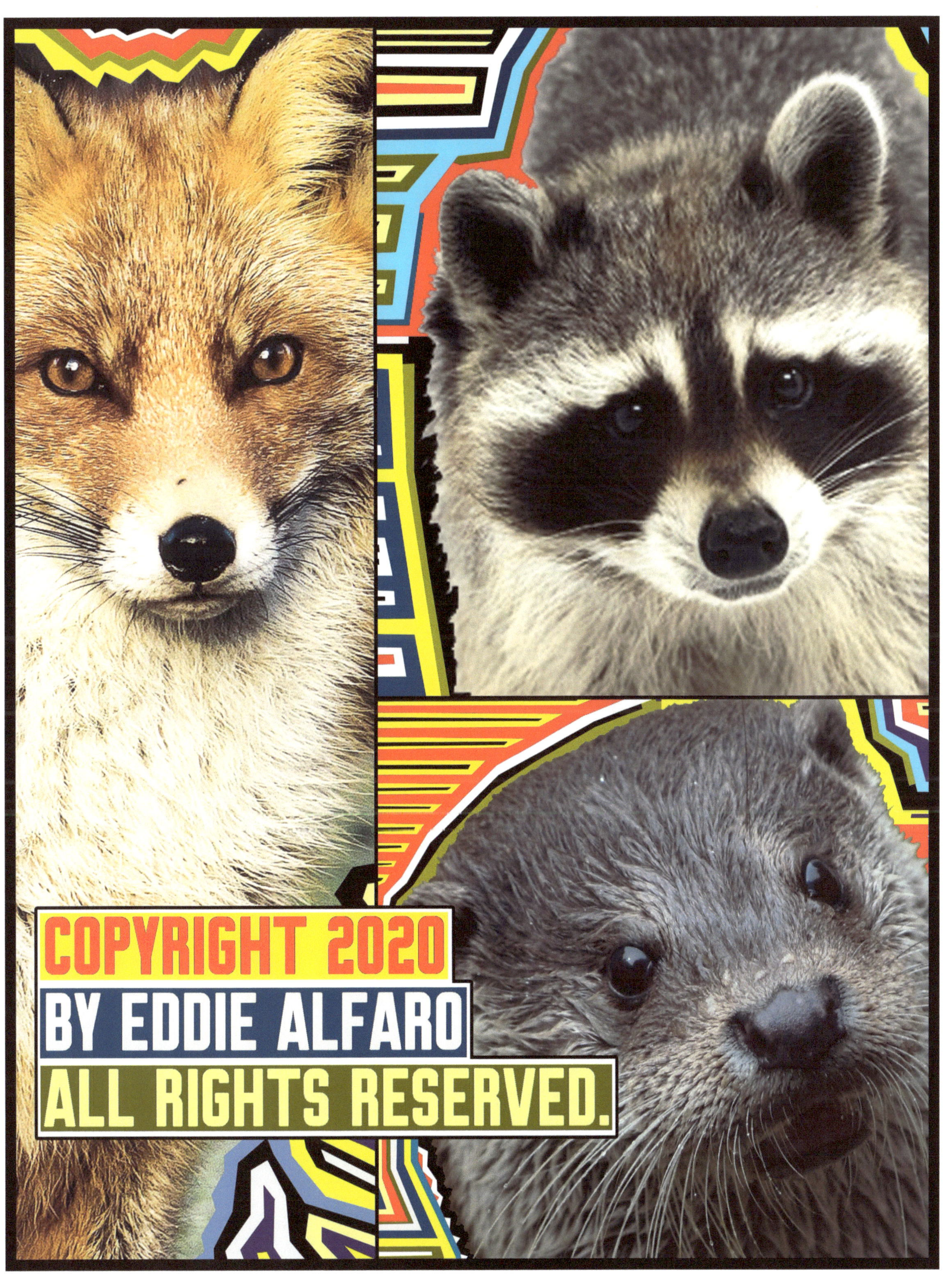
COPYRIGHT 2020
BY EDDIE ALFARO
ALL RIGHTS RESERVED.

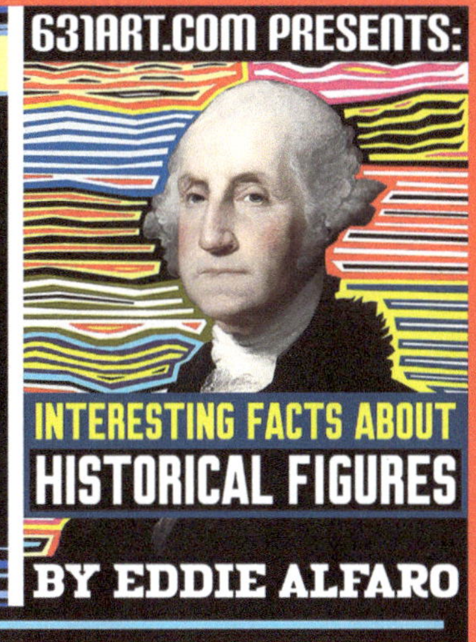

MORE BOOKS AT:

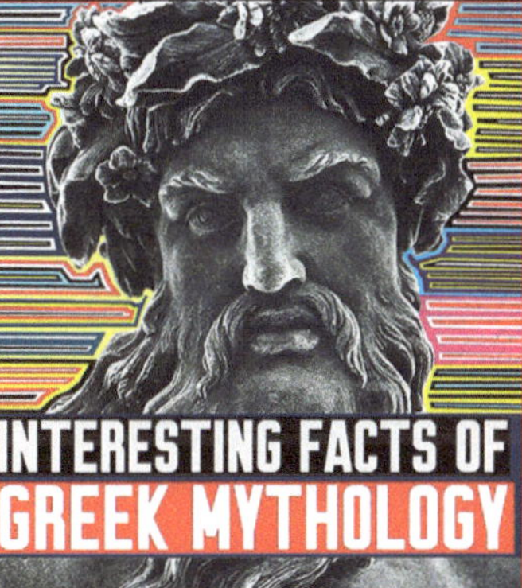

631ART.COM

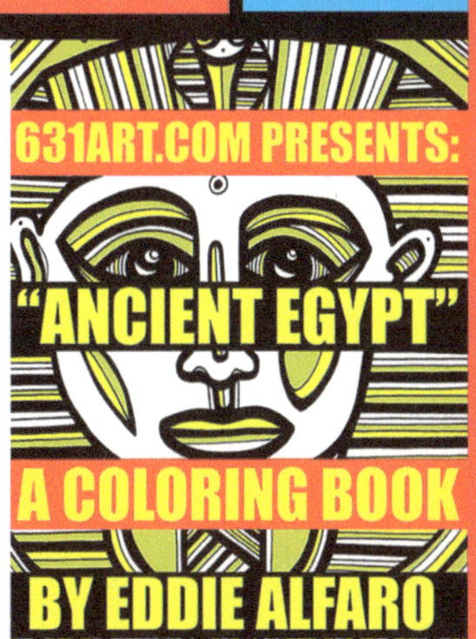